Xenia SkyNefertFirefly

Agapanthus

The Flower of Love

Balboa Press books may be ordered through booksellers or by contacting:

Balboa Press
A Division of Hay House
1663 Liberty Drive
Bloomington, IN 47403
www.balboapress.com
1 (877) 407-4847

Because of the dynamic nature of the Internet, any web addresses or
links contained in this book may have changed since publication and
may no longer be valid. The views expressed in this work are solely those
of the author and do not necessarily reflect the views of the publisher,
and the publisher hereby disclaims any responsibility for them.

The author of this book does not dispense medical advice or prescribe
the use of any technique as a form of treatment for physical, emotional,
or medical problems without the advice of a physician, either directly
or indirectly. The intent of the author is only to offer information
of a general nature to help you in your quest for emotional and
spiritual well-being. In the event you use any of the information in
this book for yourself, which is your constitutional right, the author
and the publisher assume no responsibility for your actions.

Any people depicted in stock imagery provided by Thinkstock are
models, and such images are being used for illustrative purposes only.
Certain stock imagery © Thinkstock.

Print information available on the last page.

ISBN: 978-1-5043-3096-1 (sc)
ISBN: 978-1-5043-3097-8 (e)

Library of Congress Control Number: 2015905551

Balboa Press rev. date: 06/04/2015

»Out beyond ideas of wrongdoing and rightdoing there is a field. I will meet you there.«
– Rumi

The Hymn To Isis

For I am the first and the last
I am the venerated and the despised
I am the prostitute and the saint
I am the wife and the virgin
I am the mother and the daughter
I am the arms of my mother
I am barren and my children are many
I am the married woman and the spinster
I am the woman who gives birth and she who never
procreated
I am the consolation for the pain of birth
I am the wife and the husband
And it was my man who created me
I am the mother of my father
I am the sister of my husband
And he is my rejected son
Always respect me
For I am the shameful and the magnificent one.

discovered in Nag Hammadi, 1947

A HYMN TO THE GODDESS HATHOR - from Her
Sanctuary at Iunet/Dendera (Dendera I-80)
" .... Lady of names in the Two Lands,
Unique One,
Lady of Terror among the Guardian-Gods,
the Uraeus on the horns of Atum.
The Gods come to You prostrating,
the Goddesses come to You bowing Their heads.
Your Father Ra adores You, His face rejoices in hearing Your
Name.
Thoth satisfies You with His glorifications, and He raises His
arms to You, carrying the sistrum.
The Gods rejoice for You when You appear.
You illuminate the Two Lands with the rays of Your Eye.
The South, the North, the West, and the East pay You
homage, making adorations to You.
Hathor, Lady of Iunet, Your beautiful face is pleased by the
King of Upper and Lower Egypt."

Agapanthus

Some species of Agapanthus are commonly known as Lily of the Nile.

Agapanthus are summer-flowering perennial plants, grown for their showy flowers, commonly in shades of blue and purple, but also white and pink. They thrive in any well-drained, sunny position in the garden, or grow these beauties in containers.

The name Agapanthus is derived from scientific Greek:
Agape: love
Anthos: flower
Therefore: The Flower of Love

Agapanthus has beautiful bright purple or white flowers in abundance and is a beloved addition to many gardens. It's very easy to grow and will self propagate once established.

Steps for growing agapanthus:

1. Choose the agapanthus. There are large and dwarf varieties of agapanthus, and differing flower colours from purple to white. Dwarf varieties can be used in smaller garden beds, as border edging, or in mixed garden beds.

2. Plant agapanthus in a suitable location. Ensure that there is plenty of space for it to bulk out. Part-shade to full sun will be tolerated by agapanthus. As the shade increases though, the flowering will decrease, so bear this in mind when selecting a spot.
Most agapanthus have a moderate frost hardiness.

3. Prepare the soil. Agapanthus will tolerate most soil types. It grows best in good loam soil with some organic matter added (compost material).

4. Plant the agapanthus rhizomes. You can plant them in massed clumps such as a large garden bed or you can plant them in dense rows to create a line for a driveway or path.

5. Water regularly while establishing. Agapanthus can tolerate less watering than many other plants and can thrive in a hot summer.

6. Fertilise in late winter or early spring. Use a slow release fertiliser or pellets.

7. Prune. It is important to trim off the flower heads following flowering. Doing this provides the plant the best opportunity to store energy for the next flowering season the following year. It will also stop seeds from setting in your garden. Also take the chance to trim off dead leaves and stems.

Fireflies

A familiar sight on hot summer nights, each firefly flashes its light in a pattern unique to its subspecies.

Lampyridae is a family of instects in the beetle order Coleoptera. They are winged beetles, and commonly called fireflies or lightning bugs for their conspicuous crepuscular use of the chemical reaction called bioluminescence to attract mates or prey. Fireflies produce a »cold light«, with no infrared or ultraviolet frequencies. This chemically produced light from the lower abdomen may be yellow, green or pale red. The enzyme luciferase acts on the luciferin, in the presence of magnesium ions, ATP, and oxygen to produce light. With other words, the insects take in oxygen and, inside special cells, combine it with a substance called luciferin to produce light with almost no heat.

Firelfy light is usually intermittent, and flashes in patterns that are unique to each species. Each blinking pattern is an optical signal that helps fireflies find potential mates, and this is thought to be the primary purpose of their light. Fireflies are a classic example of an organism that uses bioluminescence for sexual selection.

There are about 2.000 firefly species. These insects live in a variety of warm environments, as well as in more temperate regions, and are a familiar sight on summer evenings. Fireflies love moisture and often live in humid regions of Asia and the Americas. In drier areas, they are found around wet or damp areas that retain moisture. Also in Slovenia, we have a cheerful opportunity to observe them around the summer solstice.

Female *Photuris* species fireflies are known for mimicking the mating flashes of other *»lightning bugs«* for the sole purpose of predation. Target males are attracted to what appears to be a suitable mate, and are then eaten. For this reason sometimes the *Photuris* species are referred to as *»femme fatale fireflies.«*

When you bloom
like an innocent
white heart
in the resonance
of our love
and you scent
as an amazing
purity
of the white
morning skies
I love you
beyond words.
My agape.
My anthus.

Fireflies

Appearing in the
early darkness
of a night
indigo skies
of June
the grass
not mowed yet
growing high
hiding
ladybugs
so lovely
and ants and bees
lovers even
but above all
I want to
share with you
the beautiful
evening show
of vivid and
twinkling
fireflies.

A Heart In Me

A heart in me greets
a heart in you.
My eternal soul greets
your eternal soul.
The Temple of the Queen
greets
The Temple of the King.
The Godess/God in me greets the God/Godess in you.
I bow to you.
You bow to me.
We made it.
We reunited.
At last.

A True Sky

You will never cry
if you keep on with me
till I'll die
I'll love you
stars envy us
cause we
are the true sky
arching above
all that is
we are high
very high
high and high
high, high, high…

After Few Days

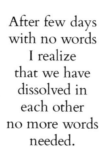

After few days
with no words
I realize
that we have
dissolved in
each other
no more words
needed.

Aksenijali

Allah gave me this love
I fear *Allah*
but it is out of my hands
will you promise me
to never think about leaving me
I love you *hayati*
I was so afraid
that you will leave me
but now
I love you more...
My God, *omry*
your every word is a poem
in every word
you put your heart...
Allah sent you for me
I love you very much baby
stay between my arms
I want you to be mine
promise me that
you will never leave me
I need you more
then you think
more then you feel
more then you believe
Aksenijali is stronger
then anything in our life
you are my soul
HoneyOmryHayatiNoorenyRohalby.

Baby

Baby
I can't wait to see you
you are my world
we are one
you are my sweetheart
I feel alive when
I talk to you
when you smile you
give me life
I love you more than
you imagine
when we talk I
forget everything in life
my Sky.

Bad Student

Yes
you were
locked in the
temple
like a bad
student
some quarrel
was
going on
but you
sweetheart
you always
miss your lady
and I love
that
you are so
incredibly
and
unconditionally
always ready
for love
even when
your queen is
waiting at home
and
you need to
control your shift.

Enkrat
bova hodila
z istim korakom
ti z mojim
jaz s tvojim
enkrat bom
vdihnila zrak
ki ga boš ti izdihnil
in obratno
in gledala bova
v isto smer in
prsti rok
se nama bodo
prepletali in
enkrat
bova istočasno
spregovorila iste
besede in
iste misli
bova mislila in
tudi
najini telesi se bosta
enkrat v
istem ritmu zibali.

Everything

Everything inside me
is talking to you
Habibti
I want to see you now
more than before
you are always in front
of my eyes
Aksenijali
don't push me to cry
I miss you so very much
I want you
more than before
your smile is life
for me
you will always be
my first woman
you are my life
my first life *Habibti*
I see you always
touching me
kissing me
I will always love you
RohalbyHayatiNooreny.

Expecting Rainbow

You are the blood
enlivening my veins
giving birth to
all that I am
embraced by grace
I listen to the
gentle morning rain
wishing to have you
here with me
sharing our breaths
and our heart beats
expecting the
rainbow over
the misty hills.

Fly With Me

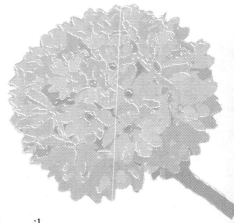

The smile
and light
of your eyes
makes me fly high
above all
pain and sickness
fly with me baby
OmryHayatiRohalbyNooreny.

There is
2.776,71 km
from
Ljubljana to Luxor
and you
are still
able to breath
the same air
with me
and you can
feel the pulse
of my
distant heart
and your
touch can
be felt even
from such a
distance.
Habibti.
Roh alby.

Hayati

You are the
sweetest word
I've ever spelled
you are my
lovely storm
hayati
I feel your flesh
your soft
white body
you are my passion
baa' sha'ek
I was waiting
for you
to say
good morning
but honey
I will now
go out
for a while
and you need to
know *omry*
that I will
love you
forever.

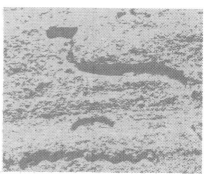

 ḏt eternity, everlastingness, for ever [noun] I10 - X1 - N35

How About

How about
real love honey
give me that hope
please don't kill
the only dream
I still have
I love you
every minute and
every second
I want your fire
to light my life
baby
I've loved you
before I met you
everyday I was
waiting for you
I was trying to keep
you always
with me
I love you in
a huge pain
I cry every night
before I sleep
each day I suffer

I love you very much
honey
so please
love me more
and more
and let us baby
allow
our vulcanos
to work together
because
I worship you
you are my soul
and please
forgive me
anything and
everything
habibti
because I can't
stop loving you
and there is
something else honey:
I never want to be
without you
I don't want to be free.

I Dwell

I dwell
in silence
because
I don't want
to miss
one single
message
from your heart
coming to me
from a distance.
I sit with
my eyes closed
and I can hear
you telling me
words of love
and I can feel
your fingers
walking on
my skin.
That is why I keep
my radio off.
That is why
I dwell.
In silence.

I Have Written Before

I have written before
and I have told you before
my answer is always the same
that I want you
you only and forever
millions of times I would
choose you baby
soft and scented rose
with skin like a feather
I will marry you
secretly
only you and me will know
if you were free
I would ask you to marry me
at the first date
our feelings are
stronger than anything

I miss you more than
you can ever imagine
I will never be empty
you occupy my soul
and my body
and it is always an
earthquake in my mind
I can't stop thinking of
you even for a second
honey I was with you
all night and
it was like heaven baby
like we were swimming in
a honey pool
you can't imagine what
I feel and smell
please baby
come to me now.

I Know You

I know you.
Your heart beat is
like mine.
The song from your mouth
echoes in my body.
The words you speak move
blood in my veins
running faster.
Every step you
make towards me
makes my soul sing.

Miss You

I miss you even
when we are together
Habibti
I know it, I tried it
when we were together
I missed you
when you were in another room
I missed you
and when I went to work
I couldn't wait to come back to you
and when you were one
step away from me
I missed you too
and if you were not looking
at me, I too missed you
I miss you every second baby.

29

I Need

But I need
I need to write
I feel much
better then
and I need to
remember and
repeat your sweet
arabic
cuddle words
I adore when
you are
whispering
those words
into my ears
HoneyNefertHabibtiKsenija
RohAlbyOmryNoorEny
HabibtiOmryRohAlbyNoorEnyWahashtini
awiawiawiawiKsenijaNefert
bahebik aktar
ashan oyonik habibti
KsenijaRohAlbyOmryHabibtiHayati NefertMyQueenSky
Love you more then myself baby.
I need to remember
the energy behind
those words.
So doubtless.
So firm.
So eternal.

I Saw A White Room

I saw
a white room
white walls
and bed
all in all
only white
and us
naked as just born
preparing
for celebration
reunion of
the two that
were once
ages behind
separated and
lived
until now
in solitude and pain
in a world
saturated with
illusions
we are close now
we know now
becoming one
the greatest
blessing
an amazing
grace.

That Night

That night
I was crying
of sadness
in my bed alone
without you
by my side
that night
I couldn't sleep
and I wondered
where have
your dreams
taken you
or maybe you
were awake
like me
and I wanted to
cuddle you
and a golden rose
appeared in front
of my eyes
I kept sending
you the
amazing image of
a golden rose and
I was planting
it the whole
night long
on a special
sacred place
between your legs.

All The Night

All the night
that has just
made a way
for another
breathtaking
birthgiving
summer sunrise
you were
planting
golden roses
on my body
and they were
flourishing
and their petals
were
twinkling in a
gentle breeze of
your kisses
and scenting
a magic fragrance
in sweet
expectation
of most delicious
nectar
that was
just about to
spring
from the
most amazing rose
planted in heaven.

When The Summer

When the summer
heat in Egypt
is over and
my country's
days turn into rainy
and foggy autumn
I will put my
beige walking
shoes on
and pack my big
red suitcase
prepare my passport
and bundle of
one dollar bills
to buy everything

from chocolate eyed
big smiled and
dust wearing
kids and I will
saddle the giant
camel of grey iron
and I will fall
into your arms
with the henna
hair full
of mists and fogs
of my homeland
mixed with
golden sands
of Motherland's
infinite deserts.

I Want To

I want to
paint for you
a wonderful sight
of translucent
summer solstice
pearls of rain
resting on a
dark green leaves
of the half grown
plants of corn
in the sighttaking
light of
the last evening
greetings of
the giant orange ball
setting behind our
hills and mountains
on the west
of the
stunning country
that holds the
word »love«
in her name.

It Is You

It is you
the man so
innocent
an owner
of
the pure
white heart
you are
invited to
my domain
to drink from
The Well
of Wishes.

Meadows

Meadows
expecting rainbow
over the misty hills
my hometown
surrounded by
high grasses
in the early morning
growing
upon scenting
early summer soil
waiting for you
while lovely company
of ladybugs and
butterflies
play with white
daisies
I lied down my back
in the bed
of summer meadows' flowers
watching the
cloudless skies
hoping
once that you
find me
you'll never
leave my hand
again.

My Egyptian Man

I so much love
my Egyptian man
habibiomry
always
trembling in passion
shivering in sweet expectation
when we share our moments
too rare and so precious
I am
the only one for you
I am
your first life
and first woman
your first Temple
the only one, and last
where your Obelisk
chooses to be erected
and we merge
in a holy union
it is a true
unification
and god only knows
where he will
lead our future
steps.

My Every Minute

My every minute is about you
habibti my Sky
not a second of my life passes
without seeing you
in my mind
my whole life
is yours now
you are my first life
Hayati
we are life.

Roh Alby

Well
samheni
I will be totally yours
I'll wait for you
till my last breath
it is my destiny
to be alone
wahashtini
to be unhappy
I love the woman
from a far
country
ana asef
you are my mind
and my heart

roh alby
you really
turn me on *awi*
I would never
ever hurt you
noor eny
cause then I
would hurt myself
even more
samheni
bahebik awi
you are the rest
of my life *habibti*
and please Ksenija
men fadlek
please
don't talk to the
strangers.

Wahashtini

And do you
know baby
that my lion
always wants to
talk to his Sekhmet
please
I have only you
don't be like a storm
I will go and
throw myself
out of the train
if it will make
you happy
oh sweetheart
calm down please
so please Ksenija
please Ksenija
please Ksenija

I am sorry
I didn't even drink
and I didn't eat
I feel sad and mad
of life even
don't destroy me
please
habibti
Ksenija
wahashtini awi awi
awi awi awi awi
ana kaman bahebik
and please baby
go and wash
your face now.

The Culture

The culture
religions
society
human laws
everyone thinks
he has an
inalienable
right to
place
their
judgments
on us
but ours is
the place
and ours is the
time
where
there is no
wrong doing and
no
right doing
where solely we
exist
floating in
pure ultimate ocean
of allembracing
love.

The Ripe Golden Heads

The ripe golden heads
of wheat
moving gracefully
here and there in a
gentle summer breeze
observing from a
distance this
spectacle of
bread birthing seeds
looks like a
wavy giant
soft satin
tablecloth
set lovingly
just for
you and me
inviting us to
come and eat from
the nature's
endless
abundance.

The Space between

The space between
my arms and legs
is empty without
you and I
wonder
will I miss you less
when I will wrap myself
around you
for uncertain period
of time
on a special
uncertain place
where noone values
what is right and
what is wrong
will I ever miss you less
habibiomry.

Ti Si Blagoslov

Ti si blagoslov
v mojem življenju
ti si duša, zaradi
katere diham
stojiš pred
mojimi očmi
daješ mi pogum
moje strahove
spreminjaš v upanje
moje bolezni
izginjajo, se
spreminjajo v uspeh
s svojimi poljubi
me blagoslavljaš
zaradi tebe, ki si
moj oblak
moje srce postaja
bolj zeleno
in je kot nebesa
in ti si angel
ki seje upanje
ljubezen je ključ
srce bo preživelo
zeleno
zalito
s tvojimi solzami
ljubezni.

We Are Neverending

Miss the sound
of your heart
when I whisper
words of sweet
tenderness
in your ear
miss the light of
your smile
beaming from
your eyes
when I plant
the flowers
of love
into our
neverending
presence.

We Belong

We belong to
each other baby
please don't resist
I love you
can you tell
are you only mine
from the bottom
of your heart
cause I want
to marry you
will you be mine
till your last breath
and I'll be yours
till I die.

When You Will

When you will
be swimming
in the emerald
chrystal clear sea
around the
islands of
Dalmatia
do have in mind *habibti*
that I am the
Water
surrounding you
penetrating
through every
smallest and
most hidden
cell of your body
that I am the Sun

drying you and
warming you
and I am the Air
saturated with an
amazing scent of
Dalmatian
violet
lavander
fields
everything for you
to make you
undoubtedly
feel that I am
all the time
inside you
and all
around you.

Would You

Would you
marry me
my heart
exploded
bamot feeki
you are my
Nefert
The Beautiful
bahebik ya roh alby
The *Neter* wants
His *Nefert*
I love you
like the Earth
loves the Sun
I love you as
the fields
love the rain
I want to give you
my soul and my breath
my mind and my heart
my body and my spirit
my smile and my laughs
my eyes to see more
my ears to hear more
everything I had and have
only for you
bahebik
awi awi awi.

You Are

You are
my world
but now you
are blind
your anger
deludes you
I don't have place
even inside
your heart
you became my
whole life
please come into
my heart and stay
forever
I give you
my soul and
my heart and
my strength
I give you
my name
my past and future

everything I ever had
is yours darling
baby
habibti
last night was the
night of the life
even during the sleep
I talk to you
every second I feel you
and want you
I will always have
a hope that we will
be together one day
you should feel
that
I am totally yours
roh alby
I will love you till
my death
please stay within my
arms
Omry.
Roh alby.
Hayati.

You Are The Blessing

You are the blessing
that came to my life
from a country
green and wooded
you're the soul that makes
my breath vivid
the image of you
in front of my eyes
never fades
you make me brave
you turn my fears into hope
you turn my illness
into success
with your kisses
you bless me more

you're the clouds full of water
raining into
my veins and
make my heart green
it is now heaven
and you're the angel
planting hope
love is the key
heart will survive
with your love tears
I miss your eyes
your smile
makes me fly high
above all pain and sickness
fly with me baby
OmryHayatiRohalbyNooreny.

You Know

You know
It's just came to
my mind *habibti*
and to my heart
that you are
my angel mermaid
sweety *roh alby omry*
one dream with you
one life
one body
one love
and one heart
I was waiting for
you all my life
we are incredible
together.

You Know That I Choose You

You know that I choose you
If I would choose
millions of times
it will always be you
my rose
soft and fragrant
with skin
like feathers
on my soul
only you I choose
now, always,
millions of times.
It will always be you
baby
and I am saving myself
for you
there is no other woman
on Earth that I would
even think about
I can't feel
any other woman
you are the only
truth in my life
you are my life baby
OmryHayatiNooreny
not only *Neter*
all my body is raised.
I want to lie beside you
forever honey.

Ti Veš, Da Izberem Tebe

Ti veš, da izberem tebe
če bi izbiral
milijonkrat
vedno bi le tebe
izbral
moja vrtnica
mehka in dišeča
s kožo kot pero
na moji duši
samo tebe izberem
sedaj, vedno
milijonkrat
vedno boš le ti
ljubica
in hranim se za tebe
nobene druge ni
na katero
bi le pomislil
ne morem čutiti
nobene druge ženske
ti si edina resnica v
mojem življenju
ti si moje življenje
ljubica
ne samo Neter
vse moje telo je
napeto
za vedno bi rad
ležal ob tebi.

Amazing Dream

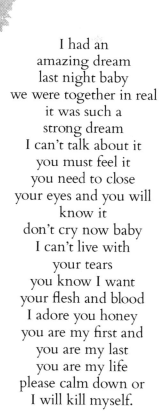

I had an
amazing dream
last night baby
we were together in real
it was such a
strong dream
I can't talk about it
you must feel it
you need to close
your eyes and you will
know it
don't cry now baby
I can't live with
your tears
you know I want
your flesh and blood
I adore you honey
you are my first and
you are my last
you are my life
please calm down or
I will kill myself.

Baa'sha'ek

I must tell you
the postman
rang
and the man came
to repair
my washing machine
bahebak
I love to talk to you
baby.

My laptop is dead
please take care
of yourself
you know
I cleaned
and shaved and
washed my clothes
and then
I talked to my brother
baa' sha'ek
please come to
my life
please feel me
and stay.

I Love

I love your body
on an empty bed
so white and soft
I will make love
to you baby
every single
second of the day
you should
always be with me
I will never
ever leave you
I would be insane
because as I told
you
you are my heart
and my soul
and I will love
you
forever.

I Love You

I love you from
the bottom of my heart
baby
you are my heart
and my soul
wahashtini
Ksenijatiti
Hayati
Omry
my obelisk is
raised for his
Queen
you are my
hardest goal
to achieve
Kalisenija

I am going to
make love to
you now
my pretty queen
please make me happy
and do it twice baby
and this is the
storm I like
you are my fire
and I know how
to light it
and you are
always shining
so much
honey.

Omry

You know
omry
I will kiss you
everywhere
when you will
walk by
I'll kiss
your shoulder
and try to smell
your hair
there is no
such scent
like henna
and nowhere
such a fire
as when the
sun gets caught
in your
mischieovus hair, *hayati*
and when

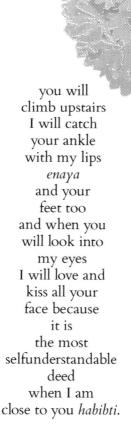

you will
climb upstairs
I will catch
your ankle
with my lips
enaya
and your
feet too
and when you
will look into
my eyes
I will love and
kiss all your
face because
it is
the most
selfunderstandable
deed
when I am
close to you *habibti*.

In The Silence

In the silence of
the pink painted room
I was feeling
the tender silent whisper
of someone
who resides in my soul
and every day more than once
makes my body tremble
despite he lives
almost 3000 km away
he makes my heart beat
faster and stronger
he makes me feel every cell
of my body
he makes me breath faster
and my sudden cry comes
so often of a reason unknown

from a place inside me
I couldn't recognize at first
but I feel and know
more and more
that it comes from the
oldest part of me
from the ancient memory
of my soul that remembers
everything I ever was and did
and I remember him
his whispers and words
of love only he knows
how to say to make me
remember all those heights
we've already had
promising they are on their
way back to us.

No beginning and no ending

This is a story about a man and a woman. A man from Egypt, a woman from Slovenia. Two souls that reunited in 2013. Their names should remain anonymus for at least some time. Because they are still both married. Not to each other.
The story is real. Alive. Going on. Right now. And from the beginning of time. And forever.

I was approaching my 50th birthday last year and I didn't have any plans to attract a new romantic love into my life. I was having a peaceful family and working life, with lovely children, fabulous husband and good work. My life was nice, good, including meditation, long walks in the neighbouring forest, gardening. I thought I had forever passed the drama of romantic love and had found peace in my heart and soul.
Well, I was mistaken.
He was sent to me for the reason that I don't totally recognize yet. But I was not looking for him, and he was not looking for me. But we met anyway. As facebook friends. A young Egyptian at his 33 years, and a Slovenian woman whose teen years was far behind her. I have loved you before I knew you, he said to me.
And we have been thoroughly shaking each other's lives since then.
I haven't stopped asking myself and the Universe, why this happened to us, until now.
But I am going to stop. Because simply, the answer dwells somewhere that me or he can't see, yet. With time, we will know. Now we learn, how to go with the flow. How to not suffer too much for being apart, living in different distant countries. Being of different cultures. Totally different in every aspect of our outer illusional lives. But in the very core of us,

we are one. We both recognized, how sacred and precious gift we have been given by finding each other, and how divine our love is. That we finally met after thousands, millions of years when the Source divided one spark into two. And gave them two bodies, and soul remained the same, just each physical body got his half.

And then we met, in real life, on the ground of Motherland.

And my peaceful life dissapeared like a soap bubble.

Since our meeting in April 2013, I have a double heart, and he does as well. My heart beats two times strongly and also faster then before. I haven't visited a doctor about this, and what should I say? That I met my twin flame and we reunited and therefore my heart beats with double power?

And there is number 13...

Number 13 has a special place in my life.

Most of my life I live in a house with a number 13. My life was ones saved in a hospital, in a room Nr. 13. Last year I met my soulflame, so in 2013. And today is Friday, June 13th 2014, it is the only Friday 13th in this year, and there is a Full moon, and a Mercury retrograde to complete the story.

And there is more. Numerologically, June 13th 2014 gives number 8. The number of my birth date gives number 8, and the number of my soulflame's date of birth also gives number 8. Number 8 is also the symbol of eternity. That is why it appears under every poem. Because every poem is coming from my flame's and my heart and soul, and they are eternal, and we both as eternal beings finally found each other. And will not leave each other's hand until the end of times.

I hope that every dear reader will feel in her/his heart, what my flame and I are giving out to the world. All of those poems we could jelously save for ourselves and treasure them as the diamonds of our hearts for the rest of our days. It would be totally good for us. Still, time is ripe to show the world, how incredibly deep feelings can arise between two people living far away from each other, how the energy of each other can be felt in a physical body, and how impossible it is to control all of it with the mind. We both tried that. There was a time we were avoiding each other, accusing each other of many different things, felt angry, depressed, tried to detach and avoided every communication. But it didn't work for none of us. And with time, we surrendered. Our minds lost the battle with our hearts. And so be it. Let it be. The big change and transformation started. We are on our adventure and we go with a flow. After all, the Source has arranged everything. I trust all his and mine decisions will be done for the highest good of both of us and for the highest good of our families and all involved. I trust our guides to lead us safely and in a right direction.

And there is a second reason to publish those poems.
It is one step further to live our truth. The truth that we feel in our hearts. We can't and don't want to hide forever. We want to be free in showing who we truly are, how we feel and think, without being afraid of how our families will react to it and without any fears from society, culture etc. Because as every human being we have a right to live from our hearts. We are each other's truth.

Review

Reading is my great everlasting passion. Some books have touched me deeply, and some have only crossed my way to get a message important for my personal and spiritual growth. But, when I was reading my friend Xenia's poems... my soul met the total silence of sacredness emanating from her every Word.

The Ones guided to read Xenia's poems, so amazingly sensitive and powerful at the same time, will feel the deepness and power of messages at the very first glance. And if One allows her Words to penetrate deeper, something will happen...

In one single breath, an indescribable fusion of Allembracing Truth, Passion long forgotten, ancient Wisdom and Eternal Flame of Love takes place. One experiences worshipping and gratitude and can't decide which one is stronger. Most of us enjoy only modest drops of love until we experience The Great One. But, when it touches our hearts and souls only for a moment, nothing will ever be as it used to be.

Xenia has mastered her ability to express the most hidden and often indescribable heart and soul felt emotions with words which can only be put on a paper by a soul that recognizes, knows, dwells in a reunion with another soul.

Xenia holds a very special place in my life and heart and I am very grateful for that.

I wish that the whole world reads her poems. Why...

Because it is Time... that Love reigns the Universe.

Vesna Kravcar

Table of contents

Cip

Xenia SkyNefertFirefly
Agapanthus

Proofread by:
Xenia SkyNefertFirefly

Photos by:
Xenia SkyNefertFirefly, self publisher,
Ljubljana 2014

Design:
Damijan Gaube

Print:
Balboapress

Printed in the United States
By Bookmasters